samuel taylor coleridge

THE RIME OF THE ANCIENT MARINER

adapted and illustrated by
dean motter

lettered by
willie schubert

CLASSICS ILLUSTRATED

BERKLEY/FIRST PUBLISHING

One of the most intense and memorable of the world's poems, Samuel Taylor Coleridge's **The Rime of the Ancient Mariner** had its origins in the accounts of sea voyages the poet avidly read, and in a friend's horrifying nightmare of a ship manned by a ghostly crew. Coleridge was a Romantic; in writing his epic, he set out to construct a tale in which the supernatural would seem real. To accomplish this purpose, he decided to lead the reader through a gradual transition from physical reality to the spirit world, and he chose the ballad as a familiar form which would anchor the poem in the here-and-now. In the mariner's voyage from guilt to redemption, Coleridge also infused the poem with another of the tenets of Romanticism: the natural kinship between man and all living creatures. The poet began work on his masterpiece in 1798, during the idyllic period he spent living and working intimately with fellow poets William Wordsworth and Wordworth's sister, Dorothy. Originally started as a collaboration between the two men, Coleridge ended up writing **The Rime of the Ancient Mariner** himself, in four rigorous months of sustained effort, after Wordsworth dropped out to concentrate on his own work. The finished poem was first published in 1798 in *Lyrical Ballads,* a collection of pieces by Coleridge and the Wordsworths that initially met with an adverse critical reception — probably because the works represented such a radical departure from the era's literary norm of stoic, practical realism. Some writers, however, recognized in the collection a fresh, exciting, new style, and were quick to emulate it; Coleridge now is acknowledged as one of the originators of the English Romantic movement. In 1817, Coleridge added a prose polish to **The Rime of the Ancient Mariner** when he included the epic in his collection Sibylline Leaves. Even though modern critics dispute the poem's meaning — it's been called everything from a Christian allegory to a drug-induced hallucination — all agree that **The Rime of the Ancient Mariner** is a hauntingly beautiful work of poetry.

The Rime of the Ancient Mariner
Classics Illustrated, Number 24

Wade Roberts, Editorial Director
Mike McCormick, Art Director

Kurt Goldzung, Creative Director
Valarie Jones, Editor

PRINTING HISTORY
1st edition published May 1991

For information, address: First Publishing, Inc., 435 North LaSalle St., Chicago, Illinois 60610.

ISBN 0-425-12763-X

Distributed by Berkley Sales & Marketing, a division of The Berkley Publishing Group, 200 Madison Avenue, New York, New York 10016.

Printed in the United States of America
1 2 3 4 5 6 7 8 9 0

Part the First

HE HOLDS HIM WITH HIS GLITTERING EYE--
THE WEDDING-GUEST STOOD STILL,
AND LISTENS LIKE A THREE YEARS' CHILD:
THE MARINER HATH HIS WILL.

THE WEDDING-GUEST
SAT ON A STONE!
HE CANNOT CHOOSE
BUT HEAR;

AND THUS SPAKE ON
THAT ANCIENT MAN,
THE BRIGHT-EYED
MARINER.

"THE SHIP WAS CHEERED,
THE HARBOR CLEARED,

"MERRILY DID WE DROP
BELOW THE KIRK, BELOW THE HILL,
BELOW THE LIGHT-HOUSE TOP."

"THE SUN CAME UP UPON THE LEFT,
OUT OF THE SEA CAME HE!
AND HE SHONE BRIGHT, AND ON THE RIGHT
WENT DOWN INTO THE SEA.

"HIGHER AND HIGHER EVERY DAY,
TILL OVER THE MAST AT NOON--"

THE WEDDING-GUEST
HERE BEAT HIS BREAST,
FOR HE HEARD
THE LOUD BASSOON.

THE BRIDE HATH PACED INTO THE HALL,
RED AS A ROSE IS SHE;
NODDING THEIR HEADS BEFORE HER GOES
THE MERRY MINSTRELSY.

THE WEDDING-GUEST
HE BEAT HIS BREAST,
YET HE CANNOT CHOOSE
BUT HEAR;

AND THUS SPAKE ON
THAT ANCIENT MAN,
THE BRIGHT-EYED
MARINER.

"AND NOW THE STORM-BLAST CAME, AND HE WAS TYRANNOUS AND STRONG:"

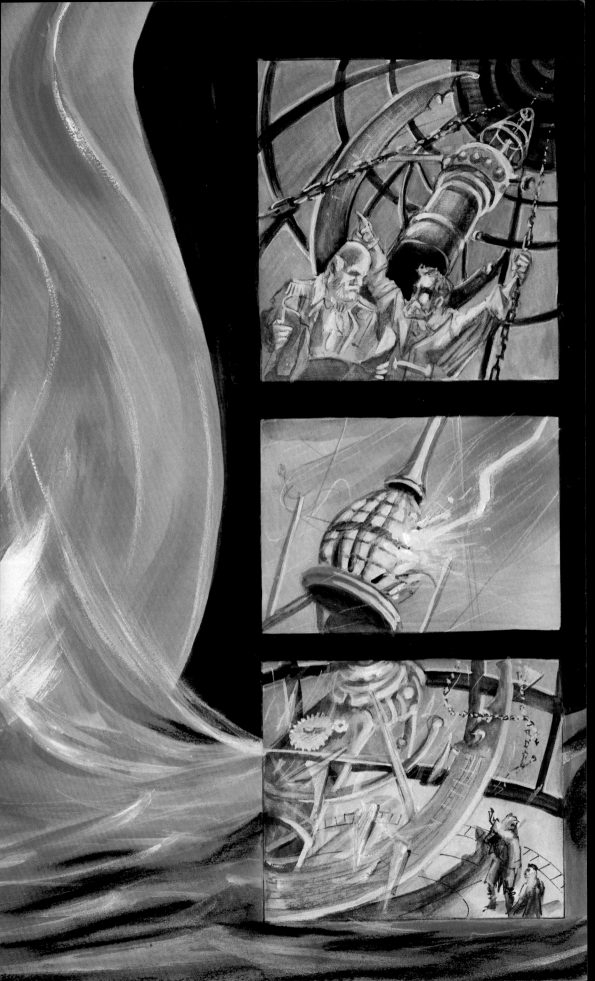

"HE STRUCK WITH HIS O'ERTAKING WINGS, AND CHASED US SOUTH ALONG."

"WITH SLOPING MASTS AND DIPPING PROW,
AS WHO PURSUED WITH YELL AND BLOW
STILL TREADS THE SHADOW OF HIS FOE,

"AND FORWARD BENDS HIS HEAD,
THE SHIP DROVE FAST,
LOUD ROARED THE BLAST,
AND SOUTHWARD AYE WE FLED.

"AND NOW THERE CAME
BOTH MIST AND SNOW,
AND IT GREW WONDROUS COLD:
AND ICE, MAST-HIGH,
CAME FLOATING BY,
AS GREEN AS EMERALD.

"AND THROUGH THE DRIFTS THE SNOWY CLIFTS
DID SEND A DISMAL SHEEN:
NOR SHAPES OF MEN NOR BEASTS WE KEN--
THE ICE WAS ALL BETWEEN.

"THE ICE WAS HERE,
THE ICE WAS THERE,
THE ICE WAS ALL AROUND:
IT CRACKED AND GROWLED,
AND ROARED AND HOWLED,
LIKE NOISES IN A SWOUND!"

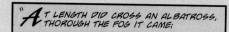

"AT LENGTH DID CROSS AN ALBATROSS,
THOROUGH THE FOG IT CAME;

"AS IF IT HAD BEEN
A CHRISTIAN SOUL,
WE HAILED IT IN
GOD'S NAME.

"IT ATE THE FOOD
IT NE'ER HAD EAT,
AND ROUND AND ROUND
IT FLEW.

"THE ICE DID SPLIT
WITH A THUNDER-FIT;
THE HELMSMAN STEERED
US THROUGH!

"AND A GOOD SOUTH WIND
SPRUNG UP BEHIND;
THE ALBATROSS DID FOLLOW,
AND EVERY DAY,
FOR FOOD OR PLAY,
CAME TO THE MARINERS'
HOLLO!

"IN MIST OR CLOUD,
ON MAST OR SHROUD,
IT PERCHED FOR VESPERS NINE;
WHILES ALL THE NIGHT,
THROUGH FOG-SMOKE WHITE,
GLIMMERED THE WHITE
MOON-SHINE."

"'GOD SAVE THEE, ANCIENT MARINER! FROM THE FIENDS, THAT PLAGUE THEE THUS!--

"'WHY LOOK'ST THOU SO?'-- WITH MY CROSS-BOW

"I SHOT THE ALBATROSS."

Part the Second

"THE SUN NOW ROSE UPON THE RIGHT: OUT OF THE SEA CAME HE, STILL HID IN MIST, AND ON THE LEFT WENT DOWN INTO THE SEA.

"AND THE GOOD SOUTH WIND STILL BLEW BEHIND, BUT NO SWEET BIRD DID FOLLOW, NOR ANY DAY FOR FOOD OR PLAY CAME TO THE MARINERS' HOLLO!

"AND I HAD DONE A HELLISH THING, AND IT WOULD WORK 'EM WOE:

"FOR ALL AVERRED, I HAD KILLED THE BIRD THAT MADE THE BREEZE TO BLOW.

"AH WRETCH! SAID THEY, THE BIRD TO SLAY, THAT MADE THE BREEZE TO BLOW!

"NOR DIM NOR RED, LIKE GOD'S OWN HEAD, THE GLORIOUS SUN UPRIST:

"THEN ALL AVERRED, I HAD KILLED THE BIRD THAT BROUGHT THE FOG AND MIST.

"TWAS RIGHT, SAID THEY, SUCH BIRDS TO SLAY, THAT BRING THE FOG AND MIST."

"THE FAIR BREEZE BLEW, THE WHITE FOAM FLEW, THE FURROW FOLLOWED FREE;

"WE WERE THE FIRST THAT EVER BURST INTO THAT SILENT SEA.

"DOWN DROPT THE BREEZE, THE SAILS DROPT DOWN, 'TWAS SAD AS SAD COULD BE;

"AND WE DID SPEAK ONLY TO BREAK THE SILENCE OF THE SEA!

"ALL IN A HOT AND COPPER SKY, THE BLOODY SUN, AT NOON, RIGHT UP ABOVE THE MAST DID STAND, NO BIGGER THAN THE MOON."

"DAY AFTER DAY, DAY AFTER DAY, WE STUCK, NOR BREATH NOR MOTION AS IDLE AS A PAINTED SHIP UPON A PAINTED OCEAN.

"WATER, WATER, EVERY WHERE, AND ALL THE BOARDS DID SHRINK; WATER, WATER, EVERY WHERE, NOR ANY DROP TO DRINK."

"THE VERY DEEP DID ROT: O CHRIST!
THAT EVER THIS SHOULD BE!
YEA, SLIMY THINGS DID CRAWL WITH LEGS
UPON THE SLIMY SEA.

"ABOUT, ABOUT, IN REEL AND ROUT,
THE DEATH-FIRES DANCED AT NIGHT;
THE WATER, LIKE A WITCH'S OILS,
BURNT GREEN, AND BLUE AND WHITE.

"AND SOME IN DREAMS ASSURED WERE
OF THE SPIRIT THAT PLAGUED US SO:
NINE FATHOM DEEP HE HAD FOLLOWED US
FROM THE LAND OF MIST AND SNOW."

Part the Third

"THERE PASSED A WEARY TIME. EACH THROAT
WAS PARCHED, AND GLAZED EACH EYE.
A WEARY TIME! A WEARY TIME!
HOW GLAZED EACH WEARY EYE,
WHEN LOOKING WESTWARD, I BEHELD
A SOMETHING IN THE SKY.

"AT FIRST IT SEEMED A LITTLE SPECK,
AND THEN IT SEEMED A MIST:
IT MOVED AND MOVED, AND TOOK AT LAST
A CERTAIN SHAPE, I WIST."

"A SPECK, A MIST, A SHAPE, I WIST!
AND STILL IT NEARED AND NEARED:
AS IF IT DODGED A WATER-SPRITE,
IT PLUNGED AND TACKED AND VEERED.

"WITH THROATS UNSLAKED, WITH BLACK LIPS BAKED,
WE COULD NOR LAUGH NOR WAIL;
THROUGH UTTER DROUGHT ALL DUMB WE STOOD!
I BIT MY ARM, I SUCKED THE BLOOD,
AND CRIED, A SAIL! A SAIL!

"WITH THROATS UNSLAKED, WITH BLACK LIPS BAKED,
AGAPE THEY HEARD ME CALL:
GRAMERCY! THEY FOR JOY DID GRIN,
AND ALL AT ONCE THEIR BREATH DREW IN,
AS THEY WERE DRINKING ALL.

"SEE! SEE! (I CRIED) SHE TACKS NO MORE!
HITHER TO WORK US WEAL;
WITHOUT A BREEZE, WITHOUT A TIDE,
SHE STEADIES WITH UPRIGHT KEEL!"

"THE WESTERN WAVE WAS ALL A-FLAME, THE DAY WAS WELL NIGH DONE! ALMOST UPON THE WESTERN WAVE RESTED THE BROAD BRIGHT SUN;

"WHEN THAT STRANGE SHAPE DROVE SUDDENLY BETWIXT US AND THE SUN.

"AND STRAIGHT THE SUN WAS FLECKED WITH BARS (HEAVEN'S MOTHER SEND US GRACE!), AS IF THROUGH A DUNGEON-GRATE HE PEERED WITH BROAD AND BURNING FACE.

"ALAS! (THOUGHT I, AND MY HEART BEAT LOUD) HOW FAST SHE NEARS AND NEARS! ARE THOSE HER SAILS THAT GLANCE IN THE SUN, LIKE RESTLESS GOSSAMERES?"

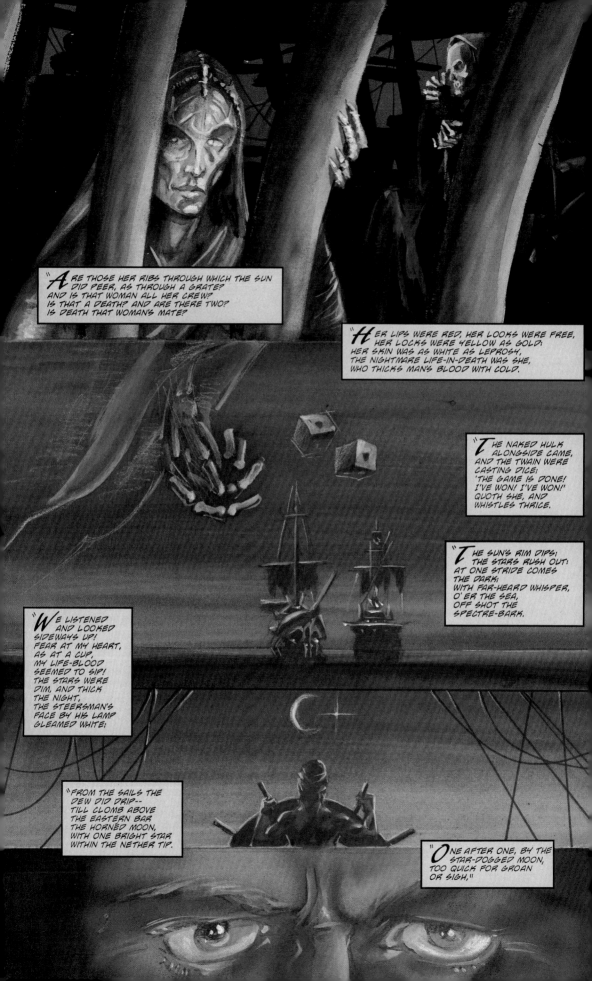

"ARE THOSE HER RIBS THROUGH WHICH THE SUN
DID PEER, AS THROUGH A GRATE?
AND IS THAT WOMAN ALL HER CREW?
IS THAT A DEATH? AND ARE THERE TWO?
IS DEATH THAT WOMAN'S MATE?

"HER LIPS WERE RED, HER LOOKS WERE FREE,
HER LOCKS WERE YELLOW AS GOLD:
HER SKIN WAS AS WHITE AS LEPROSY,
THE NIGHTMARE LIFE-IN-DEATH WAS SHE,
WHO THICKS MAN'S BLOOD WITH COLD.

"THE NAKED HULK
ALONGSIDE CAME,
AND THE TWAIN WERE
CASTING DICE;
'THE GAME IS DONE!
I'VE WON! I'VE WON!'
QUOTH SHE, AND
WHISTLES THRICE.

"THE SUN'S RIM DIPS;
THE STARS RUSH OUT:
AT ONE STRIDE COMES
THE DARK;
WITH FAR-HEARD WHISPER,
O'ER THE SEA,
OFF SHOT THE
SPECTRE-BARK.

"WE LISTENED
AND LOOKED
SIDEWAYS UP!
FEAR AT MY HEART,
AS AT A CUP,
MY LIFE-BLOOD
SEEMED TO SIP!
THE STARS WERE
DIM, AND THICK
THE NIGHT,
THE STEERSMAN'S
FACE BY HIS LAMP
GLEAMED WHITE;

"FROM THE SAILS THE
DEW DID DRIP--
TILL CLOMB ABOVE
THE EASTERN BAR
THE HORNÈD MOON,
WITH ONE BRIGHT STAR
WITHIN THE NETHER TIP.

"ONE AFTER ONE, BY THE
STAR-DOGGED MOON,
TOO QUICK FOR GROAN
OR SIGH,"

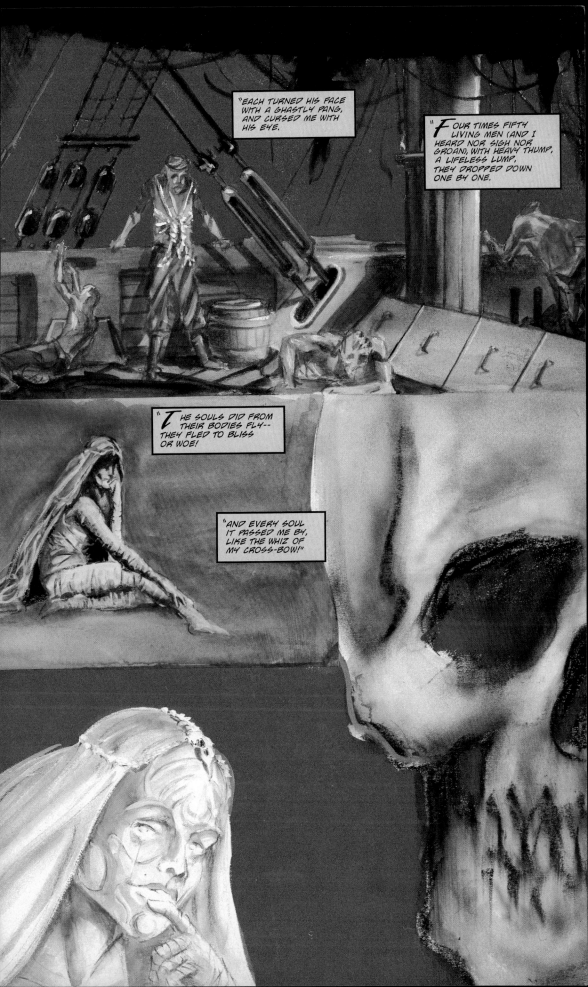

Part the Fourth

"ALONE, ALONE, ALL, ALL ALONE,
ALONE ON A WIDE WIDE SEA!
AND NEVER A SAINT TOOK PITY ON
MY SOUL IN AGONY.

"THE MANY MEN,
SO BEAUTIFUL!
AND THEY ALL DEAD DID LIE:
AND A THOUSAND THOUSAND
SLIMY THINGS
LIVED ON; AND SO DID I.

"I LOOKED UPON
THE ROTTING SEA,
AND DREW MY
EYES AWAY;
I LOOKED UPON THE
ROTTING DECK,
AND THERE THE
DEAD MEN LAY."

"*THE MOVING MOON WENT UP THE SKY,
AND NOWHERE DID ABIDE:
SOFTLY SHE WAS GOING UP,
AND A STAR OR TWO BESIDE--*

"*HER BEAMS BEMOCKED THE SULTRY MAIN,
LIKE APRIL HOAR-FROST SPREAD:
BUT WHERE THE SHIP'S HUGE SHADOW LAY,
THE CHARMED WATER BURNT ALWAY
A STILL AND AWFUL RED.*

"*BEYOND THE SHADOW OF THE SHIP,
I WATCHED THE WATER-SNAKES:
THEY MOVED IN TRACKS OF SHINING WHITE,
AND WHEN THEY REARED, THE ELFISH LIGHT
FELL OFF IN HOARY FLAKES.*

"*WITHIN THE SHADOW OF THE SHIP
I WATCHED THEIR RICH ATTIRE:
BLUE, GLOSSY GREEN, AND VELVET BLACK,
THEY COILED AND SWAM; AND EVERY TRACK
WAS A FLASH OF GOLDEN FIRE.*

"*O HAPPY LIVING THINGS! NO TONGUE
THEIR BEAUTY MIGHT DECLARE:
A SPRING OF LOVE GUSHED FROM MY HEART,
AND I BLESSED THEM UNAWARE.
SURE MY KIND SAINT TOOK PITY ON ME,
AND I BLESSED THEM UNAWARE.*

"*THE SELF-SAME MOMENT I COULD PRAY;
AND FROM MY NECK SO FREE
THE ALBATROSS FELL OFF, AND SANK
LIKE LEAD INTO THE SEA.*"

"OH SLEEP! IT IS A GENTLE THING,
BELOVED FROM POLE TO POLE!
TO MARY QUEEN THE PRAISE BE GIVEN!
SHE SENT THE GENTLE SLEEP FROM HEAVEN,
THAT SLID INTO MY SOUL.

"THE SILLY BUCKETS ON THE DECK,
THAT HAD SO LONG REMAINED,
I DREAMT THAT THEY WERE FILLED WITH DEW;
AND WHEN I AWOKE, IT RAINED.

"MY LIPS WERE WET, MY THROAT WAS COLD,
MY GARMENTS ALL WERE DANK;
SURE I HAD DRUNKEN IN MY DREAMS,
AND STILL MY BODY DRANK.

"I MOVED, AND COULD
NOT FEEL MY LIMBS:
I WAS SO LIGHT--ALMOST
I THOUGHT THAT I
HAD DIED IN SLEEP,
AND WAS A BLESSED
GHOST.

"AND THE COMING WIND
DID ROAR MORE LOUD,
AND THE SAILS DID SIGH
LIKE SEDGE;
AND THE RAIN POURED DOWN
FROM ONE BLACK CLOUD;
THE MOON WAS AT
ITS EDGE.

"THE UPPER AIR
BURST INTO LIFE!
AND A HUNDRED
FIREFLAGS SHEEN,
TO AND FRO THEY
WERE HURRIED ABOUT!
AND TO AND FRO,
AND IN AND OUT,
THE WAN STARS
DANCED BETWEEN.

"THE THICK BLACK CLOUD
WAS CLEFT, AND STILL
THE MOON WAS AT ITS SIDE:
LIKE WATERS SHOT FROM
SOME HIGH CRAG,
THE LIGHTNING FELL WITH
NEVER A JAG,
A RIVER STEEP AND WIDE."

"THE LOUD WIND NEVER REACHED THE SHIP,
YET NOW THE SHIP MOVED ON!
BENEATH THE LIGHTNING AND THE MOON
THE DEAD MEN GAVE A GROAN.

"THEY GROANED, THEY STIRRED, THEY ALL UPROSE,
NOR SPAKE, NOR MOVED THEIR EYES:
IT HAD BEEN STRANGE, EVEN IN A DREAM,
TO HAVE SEEN THOSE DEAD MEN RISE.

"THE HELMSMAN STEERED, THE SHIP MOVED ON;
YET NEVER A BREEZE UP-BLEW!
THE MARINERS ALL 'GAN WORK THE ROPES,
WHERE THEY WERE WONT TO DO:
THEY RAISED THEIR LIMBS LIKE LIFELESS TOOLS--
WE WERE A GHASTLY CREW.

"THE BODY OF MY BROTHER'S SON
STOOD BY ME, KNEE TO KNEE:
THE BODY AND I PULLED AT ONE ROPE,
BUT HE SAID NOUGHT TO ME.

"FOR WHEN IT DAWNED--THEY DROPPED THEIR ARMS,
AND CLUSTERED ROUND THE MAST;
SWEET SOUNDS ROSE SLOWLY THROUGH THEIR MOUTHS,
AND FROM THEIR BODIES PASSED."

"AROUND, AROUND, FLEW EACH SWEET SOUND,
 THEN DARTED TO THE SUN;
SLOWLY THE SOUNDS CAME BACK AGAIN,
NOW MIXED, NOW ONE BY ONE.

"SOMETIMES
A-DROPPING
FROM THE SKY
I HEARD THE
SKY-LARK SING;
SOMETIMES ALL LITTLE
BIRDS THAT ARE,
HOW THEY SEEMED TO
FILL THE SEA AND AIR
WITH THEIR SWEET
JARGONING!

"AND NOW
'TWAS LIKE
ALL INSTRUMENTS,
NOW LIKE A
LONELY FLUTE;
AND NOW IT IS
AN ANGEL'S SONG,
THAT MAKES
THE HEAVENS
BE MUTE.

"IT CEASED; YET STILL THE SAILS MADE ON
 A PLEASANT NOISE TILL NOON,
A NOISE LIKE OF A HIDDEN BROOK
IN THE LEAFY MONTH OF JUNE,
THAT TO THE SLEEPING WOODS ALL NIGHT
SINGETH A QUIET TUNE.

"TILL NOON WE QUIETLY SAILED ON,
 YET NEVER A BREEZE DID BREATHE:
SLOWLY AND SMOOTHLY WENT THE SHIP,
MOVED ONWARD FROM BENEATH.

"UNDER THE KEEL NINE FATHOM DEEP,
 FROM THE LAND OF MIST AND SNOW,
THE SPIRIT SLID: AND IT WAS HE
THAT MADE THE SHIP TO GO.
THE SAILS AT NOON LEFT OFF THEIR TUNE,
AND THE SHIP STOOD STILL ALSO.

"THE SUN, RIGHT UP ABOVE THE MAST,
 HAD FIXED HER TO THE OCEAN:
BUT IN A MINUTE SHE 'GAN STIR,
WITH A SHORT UNEASY MOTION--
BACKWARDS AND FORWARDS HALF HER LENGTH,
WITH A SHORT UNEASY MOTION.

"THEN LIKE A PAWING HORSE LET GO,
 SHE MADE A SUDDEN BOUND:
IT FLUNG THE BLOOD INTO MY HEAD,
AND I FELL DOWN IN A SWOUND."

Part the Sixth

"'BUT TELL ME, TELL ME! SPEAK AGAIN, THY SOFT RESPONSE RENEWING-- WHAT MAKES THAT SHIP DRIVE ON SO FAST? WHAT IS THE OCEAN DOING?'

"'STILL AS A SLAVE BEFORE HIS LORD, THE OCEAN HATH NO BLAST: HIS GREAT BRIGHT EYE MOST SILENTLY UP TO THE MOON IS CAST--

"'IF HE MAY KNOW WHICH WAY TO GO; FOR SHE GUIDES HIM SMOOTH OR GRIM. SEE, BROTHER, SEE! HOW GRACIOUSLY SHE LOOKETH DOWN ON HIM.'

"'BUT WHY DRIVES ON THAT SHIP SO FAST, WITHOUT OR WAVE OR WIND?'

"'THE AIR IS CUT AWAY BEFORE, AND CLOSES FROM BEHIND. FLY, BROTHER, FLY! MORE HIGH, MORE HIGH! OR WE SHALL BE BELATED: FOR SLOW AND SLOW THAT SHIP WILL GO, WHEN THE MARINER'S TRANCE IS ABATED.'

"I WOKE, AND WE WERE SAILING ON AS IN A GENTLE WEATHER: 'TWAS NIGHT, CALM NIGHT, THE MOON WAS HIGH; THE DEAD MEN STOOD TOGETHER.

"ALL STOOD TOGETHER ON THE DECK, FOR A CHARNEL-DUNGEON FITTER: ALL FIXED ON ME THEIR STONY EYES, THAT IN THE MOON DID GLITTER.

"THE PANG, THE CURSE, WITH WHICH THEY DIED, HAD NEVER PASSED AWAY: I COULD NOT DRAW MY EYES FROM THEIRS, NOR TURN THEM UP TO PRAY.

"AND NOW THIS SPELL WAS SNAPT: ONCE MORE I VIEWED THE OCEAN GREEN, AND LOOKED FAR FORTH, YET LITTLE SAW OF WHAT HAD ELSE BEEN SEEN--

"LIKE ONE, THAT ON A LONESOME ROAD DOTH WALK IN FEAR AND DREAD, AND HAVING ONCE TURNED ROUND WALKS ON, AND TURNS NO MORE HIS HEAD; BECAUSE HE KNOWS A FRIGHTFUL FIEND DOTH CLOSE BEHIND HIM TREAD."

"*B*UT SOON THERE BREATHED A WIND ON ME,
NOR SOUND NOR MOTION MADE:
ITS PATH WAS NOT UPON THE SEA,
IN RIPPLE OR IN SHADE.

"*I*T RAISED MY HAIR, IT FANNED MY CHEEK
LIKE A MEADOW-GALE OF SPRING--
IT MINGLED STRANGELY WITH MY FEARS,
YET IT FELT LIKE A WELCOMING.

"*S*WIFTLY, SWIFTLY FLEW THE SHIP,
YET SHE SAILED SOFTLY TOO:
SWEETLY, SWEETLY BLEW THE BREEZE--
ON ME ALONE IT BLEW.

"*O*H! DREAM
OF JOY! IS
THIS INDEED
THE LIGHT-HOUSE
TOP I SEE?
IS THIS THE HILL?
IS THIS THE KIRK?
IS THIS MINE
OWN COUNTREE?

"*W*E DRIFTED O'ER
THE HARBOR BAR,
AND I WITH SOBS
DID PRAY--
O LET ME BE AWAKE,
MY GOD!
OR LET ME SLEEP
ALWAY.

"*T*HE HARBOR-BAY WAS
CLEAR AS GLASS,
SO SMOOTHLY IT WAS
STREWN!
AND ON THE BAY THE
MOONLIGHT LAY,
AND THE SHADOW OF
THE MOON.

"*T*HE ROCK SHONE BRIGHT,
THE KIRK NO LESS,
THAT STANDS ABOVE THE ROCK:
THE MOONLIGHT STEEPED
IN SILENTNESS
THE STEADY WEATHERCOCK."

"AND THE BAY WAS
WHITE WITH SILENT LIGHT,
TILL RISING FROM THE SAME,
FULL MANY SHAPES,
THAT SHADOWS WERE,
IN CRIMSON COLORS CAME.

"A LITTLE DISTANCE
FROM THE PROW
THOSE CRIMSON
SHADOWS WERE:
I TURNED MY EYES
UPON THE DECK--
OH, CHRIST! WHAT
SAW I THERE!

"EACH CORPSE LAY FLAT, LIFELESS AND FLAT,
AND, BY THE HOLY ROOD!
A MAN ALL LIGHT, A SERAPH-MAN,
ON EVERY CORPSE THERE STOOD.

"THIS SERAPH-BAND, EACH WAVED HIS HAND:
IT WAS A HEAVENLY SIGHT!
THEY STOOD AS SIGNALS TO THE LAND,
EACH ONE A LOVELY LIGHT;

"THIS SERAPH-BAND, EACH WAVED HIS HAND,
NO VOICE DID THEY IMPART--
NO VOICE; BUT OH! THE SILENCE SANK
LIKE MUSIC ON MY HEART."

"BUT SOON I HEARD THE DASH OF OARS,
I HEARD THE PILOT'S CHEER;
MY HEAD WAS TURNED PERFORCE AWAY,
AND I SAW A BOAT APPEAR.

"THE PILOT AND
THE PILOT'S BOY,
I HEARD THEM
COMING FAST:
DEAR LORD IN HEAVEN!
IT WAS A JOY
THE DEAD MEN
COULD NOT BLAST.

"I SAW A THIRD--
I HEARD HIS VOICE:
IT IS THE HERMIT GOOD!
HE SINGETH LOUD HIS
GODLY HYMNS
THAT HE MAKES
IN THE WOOD.

"HE'LL SHRIEVE MY SOUL, HE'LL WASH AWAY
THE ALBATROSS'S BLOOD."

"*THIS HERMIT GOOD LIVES IN THAT WOOD WHICH SLOPES DOWN TO THE SEA. HOW LOUDLY HIS SWEET VOICE HE REARS! HE LOVES TO TALK WITH MARINERES THAT COME FROM A FAR COUNTREE.*

"*HE KNEELS AT MORN, AND NOON, AND EVE-- HE HATH A CUSHION PLUMP: IT IS THE MOSS THAT WHOLLY HIDES THE ROTTED OLD OAK-STUMP.*

"*THE SKIFF-BOAT NEARED: I HEARD THEM TALK.*"

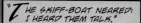

WHY THIS IS STRANGE, I TROW! WHERE ARE THOSE LIGHTS SO MANY AND FAIR, THAT SIGNAL MADE BUT NOW?

STRANGE, BY MY FAITH! AND THEY ANSWERED NOT OUR CHEER! THE PLANKS LOOK WARPED! AND SEE THOSE SAILS, HOW THIN THEY ARE AND SERE!

I NEVER SAW AUGHT LIKE TO THEM, UNLESS PERCHANCE IT WERE BROWN SKELETONS OF LEAVES THAT LAG MY FOREST-BROOK ALONG;

WHEN THE IVY-TOD IS HEAVY WITH SNOW, AND THE OWLET WHOOPS TO THE WOLF BELOW, THAT EATS THE SHE-WOLF'S YOUNG.

DEAR LORD! IT HATH A FIENDISH LOOK.

I AM A-FEARED--

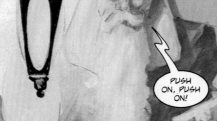

PUSH ON, PUSH ON!

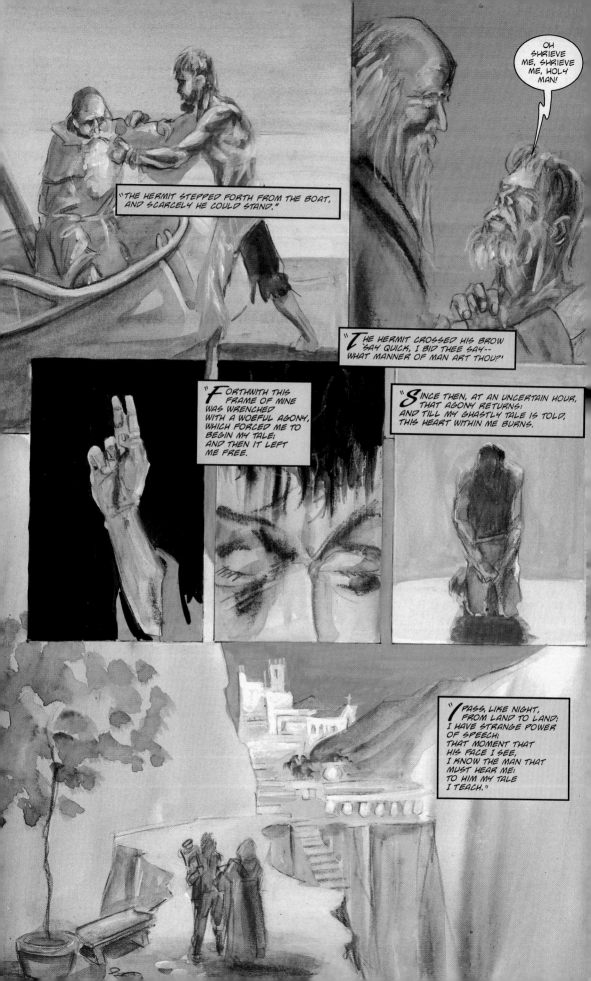

THE MARINER, WHOSE EYE IS BRIGHT,
WHOSE BEARD WITH AGE IS HOAR,
IS GONE: AND NOW THE WEDDING-GUEST
TURNED FROM THE BRIDEGROOM'S DOOR.

HE WENT LIKE ONE
THAT HATH BEEN STUNNED,
AND IS OF SENSE FORLORN:

A SADDER AND A WISER MAN,
HE ROSE THE MORROW MORN.

Samuel Taylor Coleridge was born in Devon, England, in 1772. The son of a vicar, he attended Jesus College at Cambridge with the aim of also joining the church, but he was distracted by heavy drinking and French Revolutionary politics. A soured love affair caused him to drop out and join the Dragoons; although he was bought out of the service after two months and reinstated at Cambridge, he never received a degree. In 1794, Coleridge met Robert Southey, and the two devised Pantisocracy, a plan to set up a utopian commune in New England. They gave political lectures to raise money for the scheme, but were forced to abandon it due to lack of financing. In 1795, Coleridge married Sara Fricker, the sister of Southey's wife. His first poetry, sonnets to eminent radicals, had been published in a newspaper in 1794, and his first book, *Poems on Various Subjects*, was published in 1796. He also edited a radical Christian journal, *The Watchman*, that year, and began taking opium as a cure for depression. Coleridge met William Wordsworth in 1797, and soon formed a close relationship that would inspire his finest poetry; the two poets lived and worked closely together for over a year, and it was at this time that Coleridge wrote "Kubla Khan," the first part of "Christabel," and "The Rime of the Ancient Mariner." The latter was published in *Lyrical Ballads* (1798), an experimental collection that became the cornerstone of English Romanticism. After travelling in Germany from 1798 to 1799, where he studied the philosophy of Kant, Schlegel, and Schiller, Coleridge once again moved close to Wordsworth and fell in love with Sarah Hutchinson, Wordsworth's future sister-in-law. This ill-fated romance was referred to in "Love" (1799) and "Dejection: an Ode" (1802). During this period, Coleridge began work on his *Notebooks*, daily meditative and confessional writings, and became heavily addicted to opium. In an attempt to put his life in order, he moved alone to Malta and worked there as a civil servant from 1804 to 1806; he divorced his wife on his return to England. From 1808 to 1819 he gave a series of well-regarded lectures on poetry and drama that included those published in 1907 as *Shakespearean Criticism*. Coleridge quarreled with Wordsworth in 1810, and suffered a physical and spiritual breakdown in 1813. Over the next three years, his Christian beliefs were reawakened and he began to slowly deal with his opium addiction; the prose commentary that accompanies later editions of "The Rime of the Ancient Mariner" was written as Coleridge attempted to control his habit. "Christabel" (which had been completed in 1802) and "Kubla Khan" were first published in *Christabel and Other Poems* in 1816, and cemented his reputation with the younger Romantics such as Byron. The first edition of *Sibylline Leaves*, Coleridge's collected poems, was published the following year. He also published *Biographia Literaria*, an autobiographical apologia and a landmark in literary theory and criticism, in 1817. Coleridge did not write much poetry in the last thirty years of his life, concentrating instead on lectures, his *Notebooks*, and political and religious essays. As a result, his poetic output is small, but his influence was and is large. He died of heart failure in 1834.

Dean Motter was born in Cleveland, Ohio, in 1953. He has worked as an illustrator, designer, writer, and art director in animation, publishing, and advertising. A former teacher at The Ontario College of Art, Motter edited one of the earliest alternative genre comic books, *Andromeda*, and collaborated on the acclaimed graphic novel *The Sacred and the Profane*. He is the creator/writer of the hit series *Mister X*. Motter's other comics credits include illustration for *Epic Illustrated*, *The Spirit*, *Grendel*, and *Action Comics*, and design for *Legends of the Dark Knight* and *Gotham by Gaslight*.

READING and WRITING ESSENTIALS!

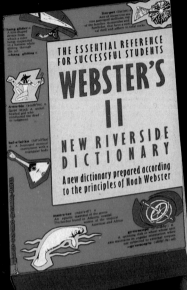

THE ESSENTIAL REFERENCE FOR SUCCESSFUL STUDENTS

WEBSTER'S II

NEW RIVERSIDE DICTIONARY

A new dictionary prepared according to the principles of Noah Webster

THE NEW WEBSTER'S SPELLING DICTIONARY

THE ESSENTIAL GUIDE FOR SCHOOL, HOME, OR OFFICE

40,000 COMMONLY MISSPELLED WORDS SPELLED AND DIVIDED FOR QUICK AND EASY REFERENCE

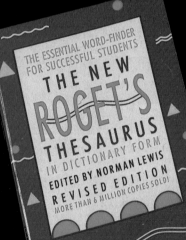

THE ESSENTIAL WORD-FINDER FOR SUCCESSFUL STUDENTS

THE NEW ROGET'S THESAURUS

IN DICTIONARY FORM

EDITED BY NORMAN LEWIS

REVISED EDITION

MORE THAN 6 MILLION COPIES SOLD!

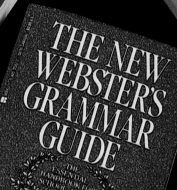

THE NEW WEBSTER'S GRAMMAR GUIDE

THE ESSENTIAL HANDBOOK FOR SCHOOL, HOME, OR OFFICE

A COMPLETE GUIDE TO ENGLISH GRAMMAR, CORRECT USAGE, AND PUNCTUATION— DESIGNED FOR QUICK AND EASY REFERENCE